# MICHELLE WIE

BY GREG BATES

SportsZone

An Imprint of Abdo Publishing
abdopublishing.com

abdopublishing.com

Published by Abdo Publishing, a division of ABDO, PO Box 398166, Minneapolis, Minnesota 55439. Copyright © 2016 by Abdo Consulting Group, Inc. International copyrights reserved in all countries. No part of this book may be reproduced in any form without written permission from the publisher. SportsZone™ is a trademark and logo of Abdo Publishing.

Printed in the United States of America, North Mankato, Minnesota
032015
092015

Cover Photo: Rick Osentoski/AP Images, cover
Interior Photos: Rick Osentoski/AP Images, 1, 4; Bob Leverone/AP Images, 7; Chris Trotman/Duomo/Corbis, 9; Michael Darden/AP Images, 10; David Bergman/Corbis, 13; Brian Myrick/Daytona Beach News-Journal/AP Images, 15; Reed Saxon/AP Images, 16, 23; Shutterstock Images, 19, 21; Charles Baus/AP Images, 24; Pierson Clair/AP Images, 27; Chris Carlson/AP Images, 29

Editor: Nick Rebman
Series Designer: Craig Hinton

Library of Congress Control Number: 2015931748

## Cataloging-in-Publication Data

Bates, Greg.
 Michelle Wie: Golf superstar / Greg Bates.
   p. cm. -- (Playmakers)
Includes bibliographical references and index.
ISBN 978-1-62403-843-3
1. Wie, Michelle--Juvenile literature.  2. Women golfers--United States-Biography--Juvenile literature.   I. Title.
796.352092--dc23
[B]                                                    2015931748

# TABLE OF CONTENTS

Michelle Wie

# CHAPTER 1

# A NATURAL GOLFER

**M**ichelle Wie lined up for the putt. But it was not just any putt. It was the biggest shot of her young life. Michelle was playing in the US Women's Open. It is one of the biggest tournaments in golf.

Michelle led by only one shot. She was playing the second-to-last hole. If she made the shot, she might win. If she missed, she could lose. Staring down the hole, Michelle hit the ball. It traveled 25

**Michelle Wie watches her shot during a 2014 tournament in Ohio.**

feet and dropped into the cup. She sank a birdie. Michelle now had a two-stroke lead. On the next hole, Michelle won the tournament.

After winning, Michelle received a large trophy. She hugged it. It looked like she was hugging a teddy bear. And she was not going to let go. Michelle had a big smile on her face. People were taking lots of photos of her. It was the biggest tournament she had ever won.

Michelle has always loved golf. She has always been good at golf, too. When Michelle started playing against older golfers, she did not win as much. But Michelle worked hard and stayed patient. Winning the US Women's Open showed that she is an amazing golfer. But Michelle wants to be the best golfer in the world.

"When you see her hit a golf ball . . . there's nothing that prepares you for it. It's just the scariest thing you've ever seen." —Golf champion Fred Couples talking about Michelle when she was a teenager

Michelle hugs her trophy after winning the 2014 US Women's Open.

Michelle was born on October 11, 1989. She lived in Honolulu, Hawaii. Growing up, Michelle did not like to run. So sports such as soccer and basketball did not appeal to her much. Golf does not require any running. Plus her parents loved golf. They both played the sport well. So Michelle started golfing when she was four.

Michelle was a natural. By the time she was five, she could hit the ball 100 yards. That was amazing for a kid her age. Michelle wanted to get better, though. Getting better takes a lot of practice. Fortunately for Michelle, the weather in Hawaii is warm. That meant she could play all year.

Her parents helped her a lot. She did not have any brothers or sisters. So her parents could focus on Michelle. Her dad, B. J., became her golf coach and caddie. Michelle often went to a local baseball field with her parents and hit golf balls. "Michelle always liked to hit the ball hard," her dad said.

Michelle's parents are from South Korea. They moved to the United States before Michelle was born. Michelle's mom, Hyun Kyong, used to be a great golfer. She won an amateur championship in South Korea.

Michelle spent many hours on the golf course with her parents. She practically grew up there. Michelle played her first round of golf at age seven. She shot an 86. That is better than most adults do. By age eight, Michelle could beat both of her parents. The next year, she shot under par for the first time.

Michelle was talented at golf. Her parents wanted to get her a coach. That person could help her get even better. The

By the age of 12, Michelle could already beat most adults in Hawaii.

coach taught Michelle about curving shots. He also showed her how to play around the green.

When Michelle was not at school, she was on the golf course. Most days, she played golf for three hours after school. On Saturdays and Sundays, she spent even more time practicing.

Michelle's coach was very helpful. All the practice started to pay off. She could hit the ball far and accurately. Michelle was hooked on golf.

Michelle Wie

# CHAPTER 2

# YOUNG STAR

**M**ichelle Wie had always dreamed of becoming a professional golfer. That meant she did not have a normal childhood. She had to practice and work on her game.

Michelle played golf all the time. She took part in junior tournaments. These are tournaments for kids. She often won. Michelle tried to qualify for a national golf tournament. Not long before her eleventh birthday, she did. Michelle was the youngest player

Michelle was just 12 years old when she played in her first LPGA event.

ever to do that. Although she did not win the tournament, she played well.

Soon many people saw how well Michelle played. She started to get lots of fans. Some fans were kids around her age. Others were adults. The media also started to take notice. Michelle was fun to watch. Everywhere she went, crowds followed.

Jay Leno had a popular TV show for many years. When Michelle was in sixth grade, he asked Michelle to be on his show. But Michelle's parents said no. They wanted Michelle to concentrate on golf and school.

The next year, Michelle won two tournaments. Both were in Hawaii. She did not have much competition in Hawaii. So she started playing golf against adult men. She was used to playing sports against boys. She did it during recess at school.

Michelle had a lot of great friends at school. But she was not so popular while playing in golf tournaments. That was because she often beat everyone she played against.

Michelle was very serious about golf and did not have as much free time as most kids.

Michelle had some success against men. But she had more success against other women. She started playing on the Ladies Professional Golf Association (LPGA) Tour. The LPGA is a group of the world's best female golfers. When Michelle was only 12, she qualified for an LPGA event. She was the youngest person ever to do that. She played in three LPGA events that year.

Michelle was born in the same city as President Barack Obama. Michelle and the President went to the same high school. It is called Punahou School. It is one of the best schools in the United States. The two did not attend the school at the same time. President Obama graduated before Michelle was born.

Michelle did not have much free time. That was good, though. She liked to be busy. She always needed something to do. When she was bored, she even cleaned her room at home.

Michelle was juggling school and playing on the LPGA Tour. Michelle's life was not like a normal kid's. She could not watch much TV or play video games.

The following year, Michelle was back on the LPGA Tour. And she broke more records. She was the youngest golfer to make a cut for an LPGA event. She was only 13 years old. Michelle finished in the top 10 of that event. She also won the United States Golf Association (USGA) Women's Amateur Championship. That made her the youngest person to win a USGA adult title.

Michelle did even better the next year. She finished in the top 20 in nearly every event she entered. She was

Michelle poses with her trophy after winning the USGA Women's Amateur Championship in 2003.

building confidence. She was competing against older, more experienced players.

When she was 15, Michelle placed second in three LPGA events. She also did well at the Women's British Open. It is the biggest women's golf tournament outside the United States. Michelle earned a lot of recognition.

Michelle Wie

# CHAPTER 3

# TURNING PRO

It was six days before Michelle Wie's sixteenth birthday. She had a big announcement to make. She was going to become a professional. That meant she could earn money playing golf. She could also sign contracts with companies that wanted to use her in advertisements. Michelle signed with Nike and Sony. She endorsed their products. She made millions of dollars. And she was still a high school student!

Michelle plays in her first event as a professional, just a few days after her sixteenth birthday.

Michelle was not 18 years old yet. So she could not play in the all the LPGA events. She played in some of the tournaments, though. Michelle was still able to focus on school. And she could still hang out with friends. Even after turning pro, she continued to get good grades and earn As.

Michelle started playing golf professionally when she was 15. Most golfers graduate from high school before they turn pro. Many even wait until after college. But Michelle was a great golfer at a very young age.

In 2005 Michelle played in her first event as a professional. She played very well and finished in fourth place. But when the tournament was over, Michelle was disqualified. Officials noticed that she had accidentally broken a rule. Michelle was disappointed. But she came back stronger than ever.

The next season was Michelle's last year of high school. She was strong on the golf course. She almost won a professional tournament. Michelle was in first place early in her round. But an older player beat her. Michelle finished in second place.

Michelle lines up a putt at a 2006 tournament in Switzerland.

Michelle graduated from high school when she was 17. Then she went to Stanford University in California. Michelle first visited the college when she was a child. She really liked the school. She planned to go to Stanford even before she became a great golfer.

"Going to Stanford was one of my biggest dreams growing up," Michelle said.

Going to college brought many changes. Michelle could not live in her parents' house anymore. She moved into a dorm, just like the other students. Her parents moved to California with her. They bought a house close to the college. They wanted to be close to their daughter. They wanted to help her continue to improve as a golfer.

Golfer Tiger Woods also went to Stanford. Woods played for the college's golf team. After Woods left Stanford, he became one of the best golfers in the world. Michelle was playing golf professionally during college. That meant she could not play on Stanford's team.

Michelle was on television quite a bit. So lots of people at Stanford knew who she was. But Michelle wanted to blend in with college life. She wanted to be treated like a normal student.

Michelle was never a full-time student at Stanford. She took some classes but concentrated on golf. She played every

event in the LPGA circuit. She was busy all the time. Michelle had a tricky schedule. She had to balance her studying with her golf career.

Even so, Michelle found time for hobbies. She liked to paint and make watercolor drawings. It really let her imagination go free, she said. Michelle also spent time sewing and cooking.

While at Stanford, Michelle met Brook and Robin Lopez. Michelle is still good friends with the basketball players. Both brothers play in the National Basketball Association (NBA). Michelle also watched football games in college. She saw Stanford's quarterback Andrew Luck. He became the star quarterback of the Indianapolis Colts.

While at college, Michelle had some of the best years of her life. She formed close relationships with friends. Michelle also learned a lot more about herself. Those experiences were something she could not get by only playing golf.

People had high expectations for Michelle. They expected her to do well in college. They expected her to do well at golf. She was great at both.

**Michelle was already earning millions of dollars by the time she was 16.**

*Michelle Wie*

# CHAPTER 4

# BECOMING A WINNER ON TOUR

**W**hen Michelle Wie was 20, she won her first professional tournament. It happened in Mexico. She had finished second several times. But this was her first victory. When she won, Wie was very happy. Her parents were there to help celebrate.

The next year, Wie won another LPGA tournament. It was a four-day event. Wie was in the lead after every round.

In 2014, Wie earned her place as one of the best golfers in the world.

As of 2014, Wie had won four LPGA golf tournaments in her career. That is very good for her age. The record for most wins in a career is 88. Kathy Whitworth holds this record.

When she won tournaments, Wie received a lot of money. And after winning so many titles, more companies wanted her to endorse their products. Companies had been talking to her parents about sponsorship deals since she was 12. But now Wie was an adult. She could make big decisions on her own. That included signing with companies.

In 2012 Wie graduated from college. She looked forward to the next chapter in her life. Now that she was done with school, she had more time to golf. And that is exactly what she did.

Wie competed in the Solheim Cup for the third time in 2013. In the Solheim Cup, golfers from the United States play golfers from Europe. Wie was the youngest player on the US team. She won two matches and lost two matches. However, the United States lost to Europe.

Wie gets ready to accept her degree from Stanford University.

In 2014 Wie was playing the best golf of her life. She won a tournament in Hawaii. Wie was excited to win in the state where she was born. Not long after that, she won the US Women's Open. This tournament is one of the five majors. Majors are the biggest events in golf. For winning, Wie got a large trophy.

She enjoyed every minute with the trophy. She even put it in her car with a seatbelt around it. She took a picture so everyone could see.

Later that year, Wie missed several tournaments. She had injured her finger while trying to hit a ball. Even so, she won an award in 2014. It is given to the best major championship performer of the season.

In 2014, Wie served as a Youth Olympic Games ambassador in China. The Youth Olympics are like the regular Olympics. But the event is for kids ages 15 to 18. Wie's job was to inspire and encourage the athletes. She hopes to play in the Olympics against other adults.

As she gets older, Wie has gotten better. Her next goal is to win all five major championships. She has many more goals to accomplish. Fortunately, she has many more years to play golf.

**Wie is an inspiration to many young golfers around the world.**

## FUN FACTS AND QUOTES

- Wie loves her dog, Lola. It is a Pomeranian. She even sleeps with the dog at night.

- In her spare time, Wie enjoys listening to music and watching movies. Wie likes hanging out with friends as well.

- *"I miss being young and experiencing everything for the first time, but I realize you have to move on and make new memories."* —Michelle Wie

- When Wie was young, she did not have much money. She would make extra money while golfing. Her parents gave her a quarter every time she shot par for a hole. The better she played, the more money she received.

- Wie is 6 feet tall. That is pretty tall for a woman. Wie was already 5 feet 7 inches tall when she was nine years old.

- Celebrities often throw out the first pitch at baseball games. Wie has thrown out the first pitch for the Los Angeles Dodgers and the Baltimore Orioles. At a San Francisco Giants game, she made the "first chip" instead of the first pitch.

## WEBSITES

To learn more about Playmakers, visit **booklinks.abdopublishing.com**. These links are routinely monitored and updated to provide the most current information available.

# GLOSSARY

**amateur**
Someone who does an activity without getting paid for it.

**caddie**
The person who carries a golfer's clubs during a round. The caddie also helps the golfer decide how to make shots.

**endorsed**
Promoted a product or company.

**hole**
The area that golfers play on. A golfer usually plays 18 holes in each round.

**majors**
The most important events in golf. Every year, there are five major tournaments in women's golf.

**make a cut**
Get a score that is good enough to take part in the final rounds of a tournament.

**par**
The number of shots a good player should need to finish a hole.

**qualify**
To be allowed to take part in something.

**round**
The activity of playing 18 holes of golf.

# INDEX

## FURTHER RESOURCES

Challen, Paul C. *Swing It Golf*. New York: Crabtree Publishing Company, 2010.

Scherer, Lauri. *Michelle Wie*. Farmington Hills, MI: Gale Group, 2011.

Wells, Donald. *Golf*. New York: AV2, 2011.